Explore the World of
Man-Made Wonders

Text by Simon Adams

Illustrated by Stephen Biesty

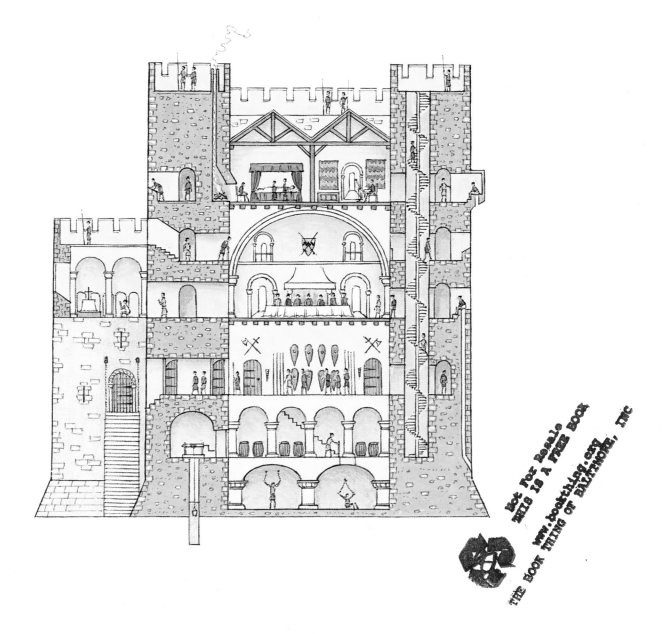

A GOLDEN BOOK • NEW YORK

Western Publishing Company, Inc., Racine, Wisconsin 53404

Contents

What was the Parthenon built for?
The Greek city of Athens is dominated by a temple called the Parthenon. It stands on the Acropolis, a fortified rocky hill. The temple was begun in 447 B.C. and built to honor Athena, the goddess of wisdom. The Athenians believed that the goddess had helped them win their wars against the Persians.

Why was the Great Wall built?

The Great Wall of China was built to defend the northern borders of China from the Huns. These were fierce tribes of horsemen who lived in central Asia and threatened their Chinese neighbors. The Chinese began to build the wall in the third century B.C. and took hundreds of years to complete it. When it was finished, the wall ran for 1,500 miles, with an average height of 25 feet. Today, more than two thousand years later, the wall is still the largest man-made construction in the world. It is built of layers of earth and covered with burned brick or plaster.

Defending the Great Wall

Along the top of the wall ran a stone roadway about 16 feet wide. It was broad enough for six horsemen so that if any trouble was reported along the wall, the Chinese cavalry could move quickly and drive the enemy away.

Along the wall, watchtowers and gatehouses were placed at regular intervals. Inside each of these lookout posts were a few guards. If the guards needed help, they lit fires to summon troops from the main Chinese forts.

The Huns were nomads — that is, people who had no settled homes. They wandered over the Gobi Desert in central Asia and were feared by the Chinese who lived on farms and in cities at the edge of the desert. The Huns attacked on horseback. They used short, powerful bows made of horn. Armed with these, they circled their enemies, shooting at them before scattering and attacking again, until the enemy grew tired and was defeated.

How were castles attacked?

Large stone castles were built by European noblemen in the Middle Ages. The nobles often had to defend themselves and their families against their enemies, usually other nobles. The enemy could attack in many ways. Siege towers were pushed against the castle walls so that men could climb up and into the castle. Great catapults were loaded with huge boulders, which smashed the walls. Doors could be broken down with battering rams. Large shields, or manlets, protected the enemy so they could place scaling ladders against the walls and clamber up them. They also burrowed under towers and destroyed their foundations so the towers collapsed.

Defending castles

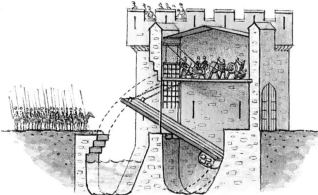

The castles needed to have strong defenses. There was a gatehouse by the moat, with a drawbridge that could be wound up when the enemy approached. Behind the drawbridge was the portcullis, a strong iron fence that was lowered to make the entrance more secure.

Inside the castle the defenders used longbows and crossbows. Special slits were cut into the towers so the archers could shoot at the enemy and be protected.

Huge caldrons of boiling water or lead were poured over the sides of the castle onto the enemy below. Also large stones were thrown down at the enemy to keep them from climbing up the walls.

Why was this German castle built?

The fairy-tale castle of Neuschwanstein in Bavaria, southern Germany, was built for King Ludwig II in the middle of the nineteenth century. At that time there was no united Germany, and Bavaria was an independent nation ruled from the city of Munich. The king had little to do, so Ludwig spent time on his favorite hobby – building castles for everyone to admire. Ludwig wanted the castle at Neuschwanstein to remind people of a medieval German fortress, which was why it was built with many towers and turrets.

More about castles

Why were castles built?

Castles were usually built as safe places to live, and were positioned to hold the area around them. Caernarfon Castle, on the northwest coast of Wales, was built in the thirteenth century by Edward I, then king of England. In his attempts to conquer Wales he built several very strong castles across the country and filled them with his soldiers. These new castles were large and well planned, with thick stone walls, battlements, huge towers, and turrets.

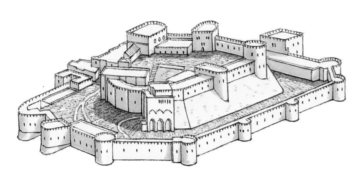

Where were castles built?

Castles were usually built near big towns or next to important rivers or roads. They often were put on hilltops, where the castle defenders could look out over the surrounding countryside. The castle of Krak des Chevaliers is in Syria in the Middle East, and it is on a hilltop that dominates the valley below.

What were the first castles built of?

The earliest castles in Europe were built of wood and often erected on mounds of earth called mottes. Around the motte was a strong wooden fence; the space inside this fence was called the bailey.

What shape is a castle?

A castle can be any shape, even triangular. Caerlaverock Castle in Scotland was built with three sides to make it easy to defend against attack. The castle was surrounded by a moat of water to prevent the enemy from getting close. In times of peace the drawbridge was lowered.

Where were they built?

This map shows where the castles illustrated in this book were built. Castles were built in Europe and in the Middle East.

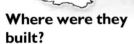

Who lived in castles?

(top) The lord and lady of the castle dressed in their best clothes.

(left) Medieval European knights called Crusaders went forth to fight the Muslims in the Middle East. There they built strong castles, waged war, and tried to throw the Muslims out of the Holy Land.

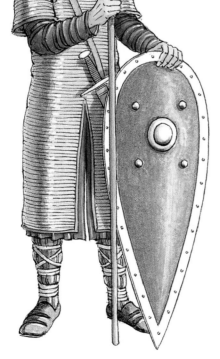

Who built the first castles?

This solider comes from Normandy in northern France. The Normans were the first people to build motte-and-bailey castles in Europe.

What was inside a castle?

The lord and lady of the castle and their family lived and slept on the top floor. Beneath them were the great hall, the chapel, the armory and guardroom, storerooms, and, at the bottom of the castle, the dungeons. In the castle there would also be a kitchen, with open fires for cooking, a well, and on the outside walls, drafty toilets.

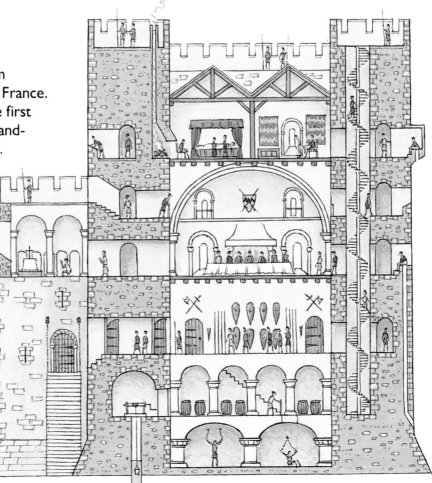

13

What was Stonehenge built for?

The mysterious stone circle of Stonehenge stands on Salisbury Plain in southern England. It was started in about 2500 B.C. and finished in about 1300 B.C. No one knows why it was built. In the Middle Ages there were legends that the wizard Merlin brought Stonehenge by magic from Ireland. Modern archaeologists — people who study ancient remains — believe that Stonehenge was either a temple for worshipping the sun or a place where the movements of the sun and moon were observed.

More prehistoric sites

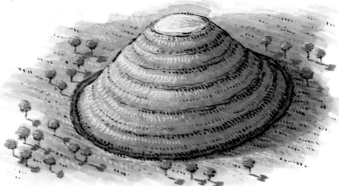

Silbury Hill lies a few miles from Stonehenge. It is the largest prehistoric man-made mound in Europe. The hill was started in about 2600 B.C. and probably took five hundred men about ten years to build. It might have been a burial mound, and there are legends that say there is a gold figure buried inside.

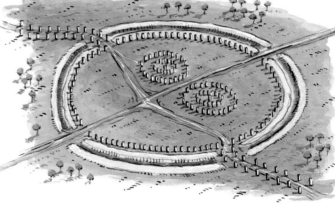

The stone circle of Avebury is far larger and much older than Stonehenge. All that remains today are a few standing stones surrounded by a great earth bank and ditch. Two avenues stretched from Avebury to other prehistoric sites. Archaeologists believe that the circle was built as a temple to worship the sun.

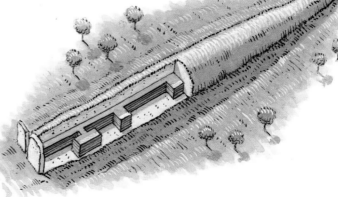

The long barrow at West Kennet, a short distance from Avebury, was built in about 2700 B.C. It measures 351 feet long and is covered by a chalk mound. Inside the barrow is a long passage with five burial chambers leading off it. About thirty people were buried in this tomb, including ten children.

Why were cathedrals built?

Cathedrals were built as public places in which to worship the Christian God. Many were also built as symbols of power, since a cathedral in a city proved that its people were wealthy enough to afford such an expensive building. Between A.D. 1100 and 1500 hundreds of cathedrals were erected throughout Europe. The first stage was to dig the foundations, which were sunk to a depth of about 25 feet below ground level. Then the stone walls and pillars were constructed on top of the foundations. The roof of beams and planks was then hoisted into position by ropes and pulleys and winches.

More about cathedrals

The basilica of St. Peter's in Rome, Italy, is the largest church in the world. It was built between 1506 and 1626 and stands on the site of the tomb of the Apostle Peter. The elaborately designed church is in the shape of a cross and is more than 700 feet long.

The brightly colored cathedral of St. Basil's stands in Red Square, in the center of the Russian capital of Moscow. It is, in fact, nine churches in one — the central chapel surrounded by eight smaller ones. St. Basil's was built between 1555 and 1560 and is famed for its onion-shaped domes and many bell towers.

The church of Sagrada Familia — the Holy Family — stands in the Spanish city of Barcelona. It was designed by Antonio Gaudí and begun in 1883. The building was unfinished when Gaudí died in 1926 and is still under construction today.

Where is Easter Island?

Easter Island lies in a remote part of the eastern Pacific Ocean. It was named by a Dutch admiral, Jacob Roggeveen, who became the first European to visit the island when he landed on Easter Sunday, 1722. He discovered that the island was full of huge, long-eared statues, some of them almost 40 feet tall, standing in rows on stone platforms. Historians have dated the first of the big statues to A.D. 1100 and suggest that the people who constructed them were all killed by the ancestors of those who now live on Easter Island.

More about Easter Island

A few small statues have been found on Easter Island that are quite different from the much bigger figures. These statues are often of kneeling figures and were probably carved by the first inhabitants of the island about fifteen hundred years ago.

In 1947 a Norwegian explorer named Thor Heyerdahl sailed west on a balsa wood raft from Peru, in South America, to the Tuamotu archipelago in the southern Pacific Ocean. He believed that the first settlers of Easter Island came from South America and could also have crossed the ocean on a sailing raft. He named his craft the *Kon-Tiki*.

At the south of Easter Island, in Orongo, carvings have been found that show men wearing bird masks. Historians believe that the islanders worshipped a bird god.

More about statues

How high is the Grand Buddha?

The Dafo (grand) Buddha *(left)* in Leshan, China, stands 231 feet tall on the banks of the Min River. The statue was designed by a Buddhist monk named Haitong and was completed in the year A.D. 713. It was the world's tallest statue for more than twelve hundred and fifty years, until the Motherland Calls was finished in 1967.

From the fact that such tall statues can usually be seen for many miles around, we can understand why they are commissioned — to impress people.

What is on the face of Mount Rushmore?

The heads of four American presidents — George Washington, Thomas Jefferson, Theodore Roosevelt, and Abraham Lincoln — are carved on the face of Mount Rushmore in South Dakota, U.S.A. Each head measures 60 feet tall.

Why was the Motherland Calls built?

The concrete figure of the Motherland Calls *(right)* was built in 1967 and commemorates the Russian victory over the German army at the Battle of Stalingrad in 1942-43. The statue is 270 feet tall and is the world's tallest statue.

Where is the Statue of Liberty?

The beautiful Statue of Liberty, 152 feet tall, stands on Bedloe's Island in New York Harbor. It was given by France to the United States in 1884 to commemorate the first one hundred years of American independence.

What are the Terra-cotta Warriors?

When the first Chinese emperor, Shi Huang-Ti, died in about 210 B.C., he was buried in a vast tomb guarded by rows of more than eight thousand life-size terra-cotta statues. Each of the statues has a different face.

Why was the Colossus of Rhodes built?

Although the Colossus of Rhodes (right) was one of the most famous statues of ancient times, no one knows what it looked like, because it was destroyed in an earthquake in 224 B.C. Folklore says that after the people of Rhodes had successfully defended their island against invasion in 304 B.C., they built an enormous statue to thank their god, the sun god Helios, for protecting them.

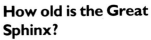

How old is the Great Sphinx?

The Great Sphinx has guarded the Egyptian pyramids at Giza for almost 4,500 years. The complete Sphinx, sculpted from a mass of natural rock, measures 66 feet tall.

21

How were the pyramids built?

The pyramids were built more than four thousand five hundred years ago. They were huge and magnificent tombs in which the pharaohs of Egypt could be buried surrounded by treasures that they thought they needed in the afterlife. Two million three hundred thousand blocks of stone, each weighing 2½ tons, were used to build the Great Pyramid. Men cut the stones by hand, using flint and bronze tools. Ramps were used to raise the blocks as the pyramid was built.

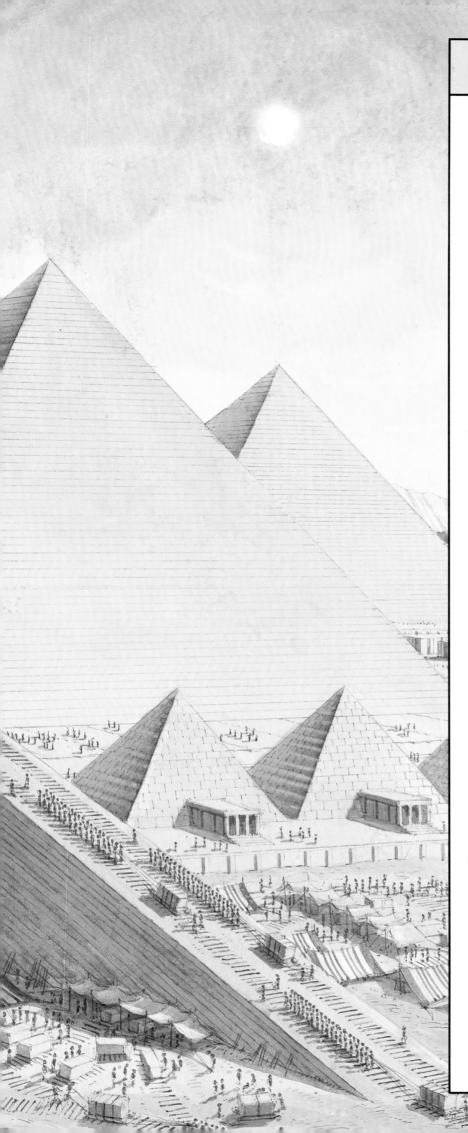

More about the pyramids

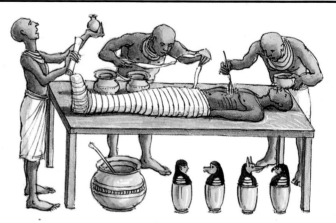

Before the dead pharaoh could be buried, the body had to be preserved, or mummified. The organs were removed. The body and organs were dried. The organs were placed in special jars. The body was covered in oils, then wrapped in layers of linen bandages.

The Egyptians believed that life continued after death. So everything that made life pleasant was placed in the tomb: Furniture, food, treasures, and even games were included. Written prayers, the Book of the Dead, were buried with the mummy to help the dead person enter the afterlife safely. The walls of the tomb were covered with pictures.

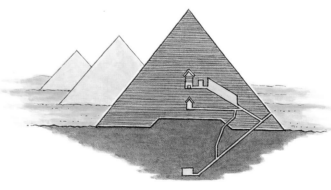

The Great Pyramid contained the burial chamber of the Pharaoh Cheops, in which his body lay in a great stone coffin. Beneath this chamber were two false chambers that were built to confuse tomb robbers. Massive slabs of granite blocked the entrance to the tomb as well as the entrance to the pyramid.

What was Angkor Wat?

Angkor Wat is the largest temple in the world. It was built in the twelfth century A.D. by Emperor Suryavarman II, the ruler of the great Khmer Empire of Cambodia, in southeast Asia. It stands outside the city of Angkor Thom, capital of the Khmer Empire. Angkor Wat was built as a Hindu temple and as a royal palace for the emperor, who was worshipped as a god-king. It was surrounded by a moat, an eighth of a mile wide, and approached along three causeways.

Inside the walls were a mass of gateways, staircases, shrines, and galleries, including a central pyramid more than 200 feet high. Throughout the temple, sculptors created beautiful statues and carvings.

More about the Khmer Empire

In 1434 the Khmer Empire was invaded and the Khmers abandoned the temple and the city of Angkor Thom. For more than four hundred years Angkor Wat and Angkor Thom lay forgotten in the jungle. Then in 1861 a French naturalist, Albert Henri Mouhot, was investigating the wildlife of the area and suddenly saw the tall stone towers of the temple rising above the treetops. The beautiful temple of Angkor Wat and the capital of the great Khmer Empire had been rediscovered.

This giant face is carved on a tower in the city of Angkor Thom. It shows the Emperor Jayavarman VII as a god-king. The city of Angkor Thom contains countless sandstone carvings. They show life in the Khmer Empire, gods and mythical beasts, religious legends, kings and queens, and elephants.

Why was the Taj Mahal built?

The Taj Mahal was built in the seventeenth century by the Indian emperor Shah Jahan as a tomb and memorial for his favorite wife, Mumtaz Mahal. The tomb was built on the banks of the sacred Jumna River, near Agra, the capital of the Mogul Empire of India. It was built from gleaming white marble, which seems to change color as the sun and clouds move across the sky. The Taj Mahal stands within a beautiful walled garden. A large pond in front of the tomb reflects the towers and dome of the building above. The inside walls of the tomb are decorated with forty-three types of precious stone. The tomb was begun in 1630 and took eighteen years to complete.

More about the Taj Mahal

Mumtaz Mahal, the beautiful wife of the Mogul Emperor of India, died in childbirth in 1629. Her husband was so heartbroken that he ordered a beautiful tomb to be built to contain her body. More than twenty thousand men were employed to build the tomb.

Shah Jahan planned to build another tomb on the other side of the Jumna River for himself. He wanted his tomb to be a copy of his wife's, but in black marble. However, Shah Jahan's son seized power before his father could begin building his tomb and imprisoned him in a fort in Agra. When Shah Jahan died, he was buried next to his beloved wife in her tomb. The name Taj Mahal means "Crown of the Queen."

What is a suspension bridge?

A suspension bridge is a bridge by which the roadway is suspended, or hung, from cables that are strung between two towers. The cables are anchored to the ground at either end of the bridge in order to steady the towers and hold up the roadway. The advantage of this type of bridge is that it can be built over a wide river or estuary without any supports underneath. The Golden Gate Bridge, one of the world's most famous suspension bridges, stretches over the mouth of San Francisco Harbor. It was completed by engineer J. B. Strauss in 1937. The main span of the bridge between the two towers is 4,200 feet long, and each tower is 746 feet high. The roadway is 90 feet wide and is suspended from very thick cables 3 feet in diameter.

29

More about bridges

What is a clapper bridge made of?
A clapper bridge *(right)* was made entirely of large slabs of stone. The piers, or supports, consisted of piled-up stones. On top of these piers were laid longer, flat stones to form the walkway. Some clapper bridges were built one thousand years ago.

What is special about the Ponte Vecchio?
Many bridges in medieval Europe were built with houses and shops along them. The most famous of these bridges to survive today is the Ponte Vecchio (Old Bridge) in the Italian city of Florence.
The stone bridge was built across the Arno River in 1345. At first the shops were used by butchers, but during the 1500s they were replaced by silversmiths and goldsmiths, who still sell their work there today.

Why was the Pont-du-Gard aqueduct built?
In 19 B.C. the Romans built the Pont-du-Gard aqueduct near Nîmes *(right)*, in southern France, to carry water to a nearby town. The aqueduct consists of three layers of arched bridges. The water ran along a channel on the topmost layer.

What kind of bridge crosses Sydney Harbor?
The busy harbor of Sydney, Australia, is dominated by one of the world's longest steel arch bridges. The bridge has a main span of 1,650 feet and carries four railway tracks, a 57-foot-wide roadway, and two footpaths 172 feet above the harbor. The bridge took eight years to build and was completed in 1932.

How does a pontoon bridge float?

Rows of boats lashed together and anchored in position make up a pontoon bridge. Planks of wood are laid across the boats to form the roadway. A pontoon bridge can be quickly assembled.

Where were the first iron and steel bridges built?

The first iron bridge in the world was constructed at Coalbrookdale (above) across the Severn River, in England, in 1779. The successful use of iron to build the bridge (which still stands today) caused a decline in the use of stone and timber as the main materials for building bridges. In America, the first steel bridge to span the Mississippi was constructed at St. Louis, Missouri, in 1874.

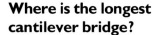

Where is the longest cantilever bridge?

The bridge over the St. Lawrence River at Quebec, Canada, is the longest cantilever bridge in the world with a main span of 1,800 feet. Cantilever bridges are built of sections that are supported at one end only by a central tower.

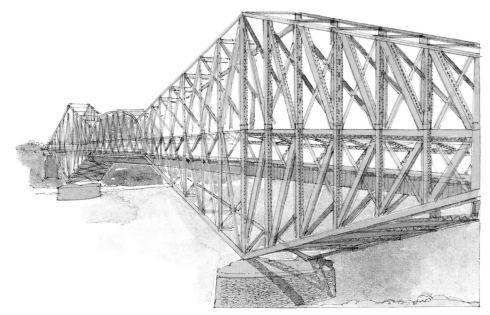

Where was Machu Picchu?

For hundreds of years the Spanish rulers of South America had been told that a magnificent city was hidden somewhere in the Andes mountains. The city had been built by the Incas, the creative people who first lived in the area. But their fortress had remained undiscovered when the Spanish conquered the Inca Empire in the 1530s. In July 1911 Hiram Bingham, an American professor, set out to find the city. He followed a trail that eventually led him to Machu Picchu. There he saw the ruins of a huge capital. It was built of white granite and was surrounded by terraces of land stretching up the hills where the Incas had planted their crops. The lost city of the Incas had been found!

More about Machu Picchu

The Incas were originally a small tribe of South American Indians who lived in a valley in the Andes mountains of South America. The Incas quickly conquered their neighbors and by the 1400s ruled a vast empire whose highways stretched across South America. Their empire collapsed when the Spanish invaded in 1532 and killed their emperor.

In order to build Machu Picchu, historians believe that the Incas had to transport their stone on ramps or rollers, and pull it up the mountain with strong ropes.

Since Machu Picchu was built on top of a mountain, there was little room or soil for fields in which to grow food. The Incas therefore carved out terraces from the steep hillsides and filled them with soil from the valley floors. The terraces were irrigated by diverting mountain streams, and crops were then planted and fertilized.

Why was Versailles built?

During the seventeenth century, France was the richest and most powerful country in Europe. The king of France, Louis XIV, wanted to show off the power and importance of his country. He therefore built an enormous palace at Versailles, a few miles outside the capital city of Paris. The palace measured nearly 2,000 feet wide and contained hundreds of rooms and galleries full of luxurious furnishings, paintings, and statues. The palace was surrounded by beautiful gardens, which contained fourteen hundred fountains and many waterfalls. The cost of the palace nearly bankrupted France and helped bring on the French Revolution.

More about Versailles

On the grounds of Versailles there is a much smaller palace called the Petit Trianon. It was built by Louis XVI for his wife, Marie Antoinette. She created a small farm near the new palace and enjoyed pretending that she was a milkmaid. Her extravagant way of life made her unpopular with many of the ordinary French people, and she was guillotined in October 1791, during the French Revolution.

The biggest room in the Palace of Versailles is known as the Hall of Mirrors, because its walls are lined with mirror glass. The Hall is 240 feet long and 142 feet high, and the ceiling is painted with scenes from the life of Louis XIV. The 1919 treaty that marked the end of World War I is known as the Treaty of Versailles because it was signed in the Hall of Mirrors.

Why does the Tower of Pisa lean?

The Tower of Pisa, in Italy, began to lean to the south almost as soon as workmen had completed the first story in the 1170s. This was because the foundations of the tower were built on unstable soil, which subsided, or moved under the weight of the structure. In order to compensate for the tilt, subsequent stories of the tower — which was designed as a bell tower for the nearby cathedral — were built with pillars taller on the south side than on the north. However, this had no effect, and by the time the eight-story tower was completed in 1350, the top still leaned to the south. Today it leans by about 14 feet. The tower is now 179 feet tall; it used to be taller, but over the years it has sunk into the ground. The tower is still sinking today, leaning more and more, at the rate of about one-sixteenth of an inch every year. At this rate, the tower will collapse in about one hundred and seventy years' time.

More about towers and skyscrapers

Why were towers built in San Gimignano?
In the Middle Ages wealthy families in the Italian town of San Gimignano fortified their houses with towers. Many of these towers were also built as status symbols, the taller the better.

Why was the Eiffel Tower erected?
The Eiffel Tower in Paris, France, named after its designer, Gustave Eiffel, was erected in 1889 to celebrate the one hundredth anniversary of the French Revolution. The tower is 984 feet tall.

Where was one of the first lighthouse towers?
The lighthouse of Alexandria *(left),* in Egypt, was built in 280 B.C. on the island of Pharos to guide ships into Alexandria Harbor. It was badly damaged by an earthquake in A.D. 769.

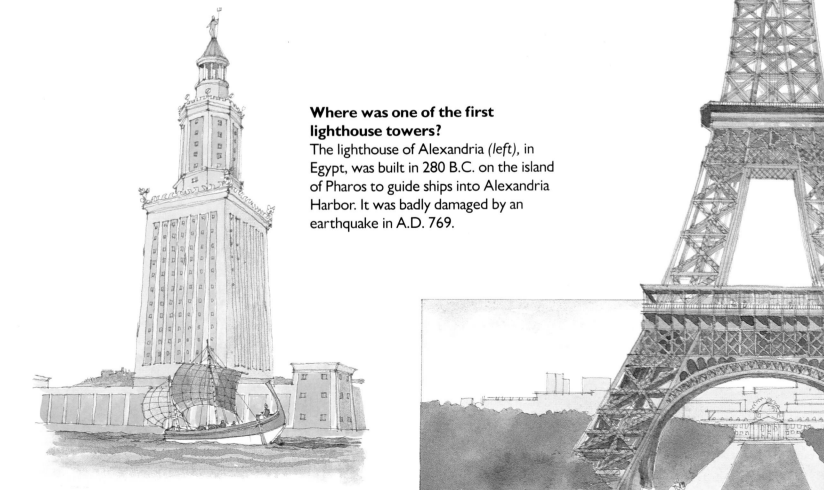

When was Sears Tower completed?

The Sears Tower *(left)* in Chicago, Illinois, is the headquarters of the Sears department store chain and was completed in 1974. It became the tallest building in the world until the CN Tower was completed in 1975.

Where is the CN Tower?

The CN Tower *(below)* is in the Canadian city of Toronto. When it was completed in 1975, it became the tallest unsupported tower in the world — 1,822 feet high. The many taller radio and television masts are all supported by guy ropes.

How high is the Empire State Building?

The Empire State Building, in New York City *(left)* is 1,472 feet high. The building has one hundred and two stories.

Why are skyscrapers built?

Until about one hundred years ago a building had to be held up by its thick outside walls and could not be much taller than twelve stories, or about 250 feet high. But with the development of iron and steel frames, architects could design much taller buildings. The first skyscrapers in the world were built in Chicago in the 1890s. Soon they became popular in New York City, where land for building is scarce and expensive, and vertical buildings are desired. One of the most unusual skyscrapers is the Chrysler Building, in New York, erected in 1930.

How a skyscraper is built

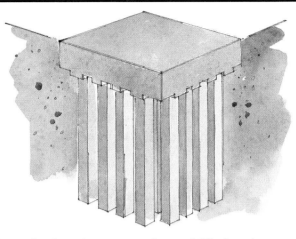

First, the foundations are dug and filled with concrete to secure the "legs" of the building and to stop the skyscraper from sinking into the ground.

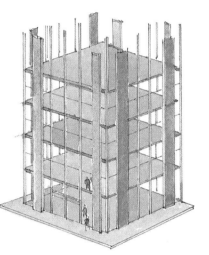

Second, the central steel frame of the building is erected. The building is held up by this interior skeleton, rather than by massive exterior walls.

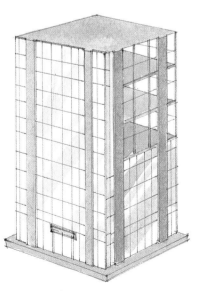

Third, the lightweight exterior walls are added, and finally, the building is equipped with electricity and other services. It is then ready to be occupied.

41

What was the Colosseum used for?

The Colosseum is a huge open-air theater in Rome where games took place during the time of the Roman Empire. The games consisted of combat between trained fighters, known as gladiators; occasionally the men had to fight wild animals. The Colosseum was constructed around A.D. 80 and is in the shape of an oval measuring 617 feet by 512 feet. Inside, four galleries seated up to fifty thousand spectators. Many of the spectators were protected from the sun by a huge canvas awning. Beneath the arena was a maze of tunnels and chambers.

More about the gladiators

Gladiators were prisoners of war, criminals, or slaves who had displeased their masters. They were trained to fight in special schools. If they fought unusually well, they were pardoned and set free. If defeated, they received the "thumbs-down" sign and were killed.

Each gladiator had a different weapon to fight with. Some fought with nets and tridents (three-pronged spears), others with bows and arrows or with swords and shields. Some even fought on horseback. The games were great crowd pleasers and fans cheered for their favorite gladiators.

Some gladiators had to fight wild animals, such as tigers and lions. The wild animals were not fed in order to make them fierce. Sometimes Christians, who were persecuted for their religious beliefs, were thrown to the lions. But they would not fight and sang hymns until the lions had killed them.

What shape is the Sydney Opera House?

The brilliant white roof of the Sydney Opera House, in Australia, is shaped like the billowing sails of a yacht. This design was chosen because the Opera House sits on the shores of Sydney Harbor, which is often filled with yachts and other sailboats. The Opera House was planned by a Danish architect, Joern Utzon. It took fourteen years to build and was finally opened in 1973. Because of its strange shape, it was very difficult to construct. The total cost was more than one hundred million Australian dollars.

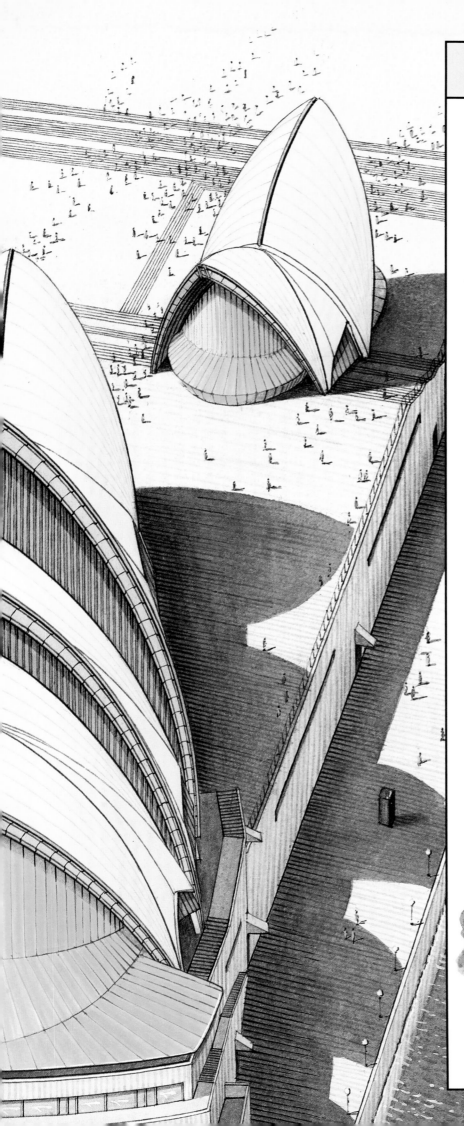

More strangely shaped buildings

The Pompidou Center, named after a recent French president, is situated in Paris. It was designed "inside out" — all the pipes, lifts, and plumbing are on the outside of the building, thus leaving a lot of space inside for the art exhibitions.

The EPCOT Center — Experimental Prototype Community of Tomorrow — was built at Disney World in Florida. The center is a theme park showing human progress through the ages. The sphere pictured above is called Spaceship Earth.

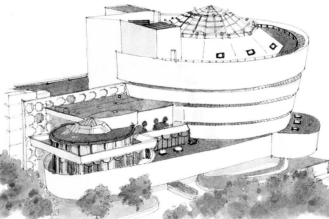

The Guggenheim Museum is in New York City and houses a large collection of modern art. The building was designed by Frank Lloyd Wright. Inside, a continuous spiral ramp, almost a third of a mile in length, winds up to the glass dome in the roof.

INDEX

AN ILEX BOOK
Created and produced by Ilex Publishers Limited
29-31 George Street, Oxford, OX1 2AJ

Main illustrations by Stephen Biesty/Jillian Burgess Illustration
Other illustrations by Stephen Biesty and Ian Heard